Grandmother's Story

of

BUNKER HILL
BATTLE

As She Saw It from the Belfry

Grandmother's Story
of
BUNKER HILL
BATTLE

As She Saw It from the Belfry

BY

Oliver Wendell Holmes

WITH ILLUSTRATIONS BY

Howard Pyle

CHAPMAN BILLIES
Sandwich, Massachusetts

This edition published in 1995 by

Chapman Billies, Inc.
Box 819
Sandwich, Massachusetts 02563

ISBN 0-939218-10-0

Manufactured in the United States of America

THIS EDITION
IS DEDICATED TO

Emily and Sabrina

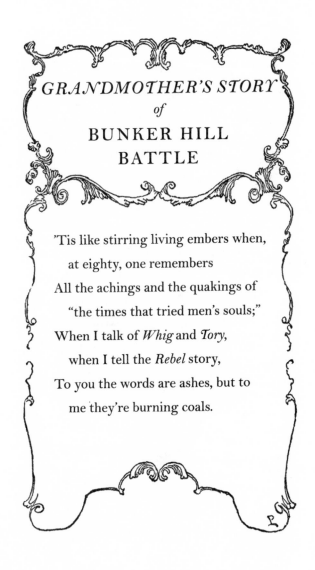

GRANDMOTHER'S STORY
of
BUNKER HILL
BATTLE

'Tis like stirring living embers when,
  at eighty, one remembers
All the achings and the quakings of
  "the times that tried men's souls;"
When I talk of *Whig* and *Tory*,
  when I tell the *Rebel* story,
To you the words are ashes, but to
  me they're burning coals.

I had heard the muskets' rattle of the
    April running battle;
Lord Percy's hunted soldiers, I can
    see their red coats still;
But a deadly chill comes o'er me, as
    the day looms up before me,
When a thousand men lay bleeding
    on the slopes of Bunker's Hill.

'Twas a peaceful summer's morning,
    when the first thing gave us warning
Was the booming of the cannon from
    the river and the shore:
"Child," says grandma, "what's the
    matter, what is all this noise and
    clatter?
Have those scalping Indian devils
    come to murder us once more?"

Poor old soul! my sides were shaking
in the midst of all my quaking,
To hear her talk of Indians when the
guns began to roar:
She had seen the burning village, and
the slaughter and the pillage,
When the Mohawks killed her father
with their bullets through his door.

14   *GRANDMOTHER'S STORY*

Then I said, "Now, dear old granny,
    don't you fret and worry any,
For I'll soon come back and tell you
    whether this is work or play;
There can't be mischief in it, so I
    won't be gone a minute"—
For a minute then I started. I was
    gone the livelong day.

No time for bodice-lacing or for
    looking-glass grimacing;
Down my hair went as I hurried,
    tumbling half-way to my heels;
God forbid your ever knowing, when
    there's blood around her flowing,
How the lonely, helpless daughter of
    a quiet household feels!

In the street I heard a thumping; and
  I knew it was the stumping
Of the Corporal, our old neighbor, on
  that wooden leg he wore,
With a knot of women round him,—
  it was lucky I had found him,
So I followed with the others, and the
  Corporal marched before.

They were making for the steeple,—
    the old soldier and his people;
The pigeons circled round us as we
    climbed the creaking stair,
Just across the narrow river — oh,
    so close it made me shiver! —
Stood a fortress on the hill-top that
    but yesterday was bare.

Not slow our eyes to find it; well we
    knew who stood behind it,
Though the earthwork hid them from
    us, and the stubborn walls were dumb:
Here were sister, wife, and mother,
    looking wild upon each other,
And their lips were white with terror
    as they said, THE HOUR HAS COME!

The morning slowly wasted, not a
   morsel had we tasted,
And our heads were almost splitting
   with the cannon's deafening thrill,
When a figure tall and stately round
   the rampart strode sedately;
It was PRESCOTT, one since told me;
   he commanded on the hill.

Every woman's heart grew bigger
 when we saw his manly figure,
With the banyan buckled round it,
 standing up so straight and tall;
Like a gentleman of leisure who is
 strolling out for pleasure,
Through the storm of shells and
 cannon-shot he walked around
 the wall.

At eleven the streets were swarming,
   for the red-coats' ranks were forming;
At noon in marching order they were
   moving to the piers;
How the bayonets gleamed and glistened,
   as we looked far down, and listened
To the trampling and the drum-beat
   of the belted grenadiers!

At length the men have started, with
    a cheer (it seemed faint-hearted),
In their scarlet regimentals, with
    their knapsacks on their backs,
And the reddening, rippling water, as
    after a sea-fight's slaughter,
Round the barges gliding onward
    blushed like blood along their tracks.

So they crossed to the other border,
    and again they formed in order;
And the boats came back for soldiers,
    came for soldiers, soldiers still:
The time seemed everlasting to us
    women faint and fasting,—
At last they're moving, marching,
    marching proudly up the hill.

We can see the bright steel glancing
    all along the lines advancing —
Now the front rank fires a volley —
    they have thrown away their shot;
For behind their earthwork lying, all
    the balls above them flying,
Our people need not hurry; so they
    wait and answer not.

Then the Corporal, our old cripple (he
    would swear sometimes and tipple),—
He had heard the bullets whistle (in
    the old French war) before,—
Calls out in words of jeering, just as
    if they all were hearing,—
And his wooden leg thumps fiercely
    on the dusty belfry floor: —

Here lies buried in a
Stone Grave 10 feet deep
Cap DANIEL MALCOM mcht
who departed this Life
october 23d 1769
Aged 44 Years 3
a true son of Liberty
a Friend to the Publick
an Enemy to oppression
and one of the foremost
in opposing the Revenue Acts
on America

"Oh! fire away, ye villains, and earn
  King George's shillin's,
But ye'll waste a ton of powder afore
  a 'rebel' falls;
You may bang the dirt and welcome,
  they're as safe as Dan'l Malcolm
Ten foot beneath the gravestone that
  you've splintered with your balls!"

In the hush of expectation, in the
    awe and trepidation
Of the dread approaching moment,
    we are well-nigh breathless all;
Though the rotten bars are failing on
    the rickety belfry railing,
We are crowding up against them
    like the waves against a wall.

Just a glimpse (the air is clearer),

    they are nearer,— nearer,— nearer,

When a flash — a curling smoke-wreath —

    then a crash — the steeple shakes —

The deadly truce is ended; the tempest's

    shroud is rended;

Like a morning mist it gathered, like

    a thunder-cloud it breaks!

Oh the sight our eyes discover as the
blue-black smoke blows over!
The red-coats stretched in windrows
as a mower rakes his hay;
Here a scarlet heap is lying, there a
headlong crowd is flying
Like a billow that has broken and is
shivered into spray.

Then we cried, "The troops are routed!
    they are beat — it can't be doubted!
God be thanked, the fight is over!"
    — Ah! the grim old soldier's smile!
"Tell us, tell us why you look so?" (we
    could hardly speak, we shook so),—
"Are they beaten? *Are* they beaten?
    ARE they beaten?"—"Wait a while."

Oh the trembling and the terror! for
 too soon we saw our error:
They are baffled, not defeated; we
 have driven them back in vain;
And the columns that were scattered,
 round the colors that were tattered,
Toward the sullen, silent fortress turn
 their belted breasts again.

All at once, as we are gazing, lo the
    roofs of Charlestown blazing!
They have fired the harmless village;
    in an hour it will be down!
The Lord in heaven confound them,
    rain his fire and brimstone round
    them,—
The robbing, murdering red-coats,
    that would burn a peaceful town!

They are marching, stern and solemn;
   we can see each massive column
As they near the naked earth-mound
   with the slanting walls so steep.
Have our soldiers got faint-hearted,
   and in noiseless haste departed?
Are they panic-struck and helpless?
   Are they palsied or asleep?

Now! the walls they're almost under!
  scarce a rod the foes asunder!
Not a firelock flashed against them!
  up the earthwork they will swarm!
But the words have scarce been spoken,
  when the ominous calm is broken,
And a bellowing crash has emptied
  all the vengeance of the storm!

So again, with murderous slaughter,
    pelted backwards to the water,
Fly Pigot's running heroes and the
    frightened braves of Howe;
And we shout, "At last they're done for,
    it's their barges they have run for:
They are beaten, beaten, beaten; and
    the battle's over now!"

And we looked, poor timid creatures,
  on the rough old soldier's features,
Our lips afraid to question, but he
  knew what we would ask:
"Not sure," he said; "keep quiet,—
  once more, I guess, they'll try it—
Here's damnation to the cut-throats!"—
  then he handed me his flask,

Saying, "Gal, you're looking shaky;
    have a drop of old Jamaiky;
I'm afeard there'll be more trouble
    afore the job is done;"
So I took one scorching swallow;
    dreadful faint I felt and hollow,
Standing there from early morning
    when the firing was begun.

All through those hours of trial I had
    watched a calm clock dial,
As the hands kept creeping, creeping,—
    they were creeping round to four,
When the old man said, "They're forming
    with their bagonets fixed for storming:
It's the death-grip that's a-coming,—
    they will try the works once more."

With brazen trumpets blaring, the
    flames behind them glaring,
The deadly wall before them, in close
    array they come;
Still onward, upward toiling, like a
    dragon's fold uncoiling,—
Like the rattlesnake's shrill warning
    the reverberating drum!

Over heaps all torn and gory — shall I
   tell the fearful story,
How they surged above the breastwork,
   as a sea breaks over a deck;
How, driven, yet scarce defeated, our
   worn-out men retreated,
With their powder-horns all emptied,
   like the swimmers from a wreck?

It has all been told and painted; as
    for me, they say I fainted,
And the wooden-legged old Corporal
    stumped with me down the stair:
When I woke from dreams affrighted
    the evening lamps were lighted,—
On the floor a youth was lying; his
    bleeding breast was bare.

And I heard through all the flurry,
   "Send for WARREN! hurry! hurry!
Tell him here's a soldier bleeding,
   and he'll come and dress his wound!"
Ah, we knew not till the morrow told
   its tale of death and sorrow,
How the starlight found him stiffened
   on the dark and bloody ground.

Who the youth was, what his name
    was, where the place from which he
    came was,
Who had brought him from the battle,
    and had left him at our door,
He could not speak to tell us; but 'twas
    one of our brave fellows,
As the homespun plainly showed us
    which the dying soldier wore.

For they all thought he was dying, as
    they gathered round him crying,—
And they said, "Oh, how they'll miss
    him!" and "What *will* his mother do?"
Then, his eyelids just unclosing like a
    child's that has been dozing,
He faintly murmured, "Mother!"—
    and — I saw his eyes were blue.

"Why, grandma, how you're winking!"
　Ah, my child, it sets me thinking
Of a story not like this one. Well,
　he somehow lived along;
So we came to know each other, and
　I nursed him like a — mother,
Till at last he stood before me, tall,
　and rosy-cheeked, and strong.

And we sometimes walked together
   in the pleasant summer weather,
—"Please to tell us what his name was?"
   Just your own, my little dear,—
There's his picture Copley painted:
   we became so well acquainted,
That — in short, that's why I'm grandma,
   and you children all are here!

Grandmother's Story of Bunker Hill Battle was designed and composed by Scott-Martin Kosofsky at the Philidor Company, Boston, based on the 1875 Riverside Press edition. Steve Dyer assisted with the production. The types are digital renderings of those cut in 1788 by Richard Austin for John Bell's English Letter Foundry, reissued by the English Monotype Corporation in the 1930's. The original "Bell" types found their way to Boston in the 19th century and were used frequently by Daniel Berkeley Updike and Bruce Rogers at the Riverside Press, in Cambridge. They are considered the first "modern" types made in England and were amongst the earliest to eschew the use of the long ſ (s). This version was made by Monotype Typography, Ltd., and modified by Mr. Kosofsky. The book was printed and bound by BookCrafters, Inc.

DATE DUE